UNSTOPPABLE POWER

JAY KUHNS

PUBLISHING

CONTENTS

DEDICATION

To Mom and Dad

TESTIMONIALS

In Unstoppable Power, Jay Kuhns challenges us to take control of our purpose, be bold and provide the leadership that is desperately needed in organizations today. His elements of leadership are provocative and inspiring and had an immediate impact on how I approach my job.

MICHAEL WUKITSCH CHIEF PEOPLE OFFICER LEE HEALTH FORT MYERS FL

This book had me at, "Perhaps never in our lifetime have organizations, and the world, needed authentic, decisive leadership more than we do now. Tired and outdated leadership styles have derailed many companies."

This is such a powerful line. I develop leaders across the globe, and I stress the same in my conversation.

Gone are the days of singularly focused leader, know-all leader, and answer person. Covid has ushered out the outdated leadership persona, and it could not have come at a better time. Strategy is shifting, Innovation is at the forefront, and the DNA of the workforce is changing. Multi-generation workers are demanding a different approach than the outdated model.

An organization needs a different style of leader to usher in this new era. If an organization's customer mix changed, they would not think twice before making the adjustment.

Thankfully Unstoppable Power comes along at a pivotal moment that will allow leaders not only to grow but thrive in the new work of work.

RON THOMAS, MANAGING DIRECTOR – STRATEGY, FOCUSED GROUP, UNITED ARAB EMIRATES

The old and tired approach to leadership - rooted in hierarchy, seniority, and backroom politicking - continues to suck the life out of the workplace. Leaders like this not only keep your people from being their best selves, but they're probably killing your company. Unstoppable Power provides a simple roadmap for helping your leaders forge meaningful human connections with your employees and foster an environment in which they can thrive.

CHARLIE JUDY, CHIEF PEOPLE & CULTURE OFFICER, INTELLIGENT MEDICAL OBJECTS, CHICAGO, IL

Having known Jay Kuhns for almost two decades as a colleague, strategic thought partner, and HR professional, I can firmly attest to his master-class as a preeminent source of cutting edge thinking and progressive business strategies.

His energy is contagious and is only matched by his ability to understand how to help individuals and organizations cut through the trivial and focus on the impactful. He is by defini-

tion an Unstoppable Power who motivates and moves people from inertia to action through purposeful partnership. This book is a testament to the influence he has had and will have on our current and future generation of leaders.

After learning about the Unstoppable Power, it made me realize that being a high energy leader every single day was a strength that I needed to truly embrace. Jay does a great job of articulating the concept of realizing that focusing on taking risks and valuing relationships is a true authentic way to becoming a more effective leader.

I've known Jay for many years. His background and experience, coupled with his personality and insights, makes for an interesting and unique contribution to the genre of leadership excellence. This book is practical, precise and direct. I am happy for you to continue your unstoppable leadership journey with Jay's insights.

People today feel powerless – personally and professionally. They're looking for a catalyst that will move them ahead, inspire them and be sustainable. Jay Kuhns captures what is needed to make that happen in his new book!! He lives the concepts of limitless energy, risk taking, and building relationships as a leader himself. He shows us how to translate this to leadership in all corners and levels of the business world. So, step up, dive into this book, and regain the power you desire!

STEVE BROWNE, SHROM-SCP CHIEF PEOPLE OFFICER LAROSA'S INC, AUTHOR OF – HR ON PURPOSE !! AND HR RISING !!, CINCINNATI, OH

Jay's approach to life and leadership is genuine and refreshing! The leadership playbook of days gone by can be thrown out and replaced with the principles outlined in Unstoppable Power - it IS the new playbook. Unstoppable Power highlights the importance of authenticity, taking risks and high energy, and Jay's heartfelt leadership style is the example that all leaders should follow!

TINA M. SUOJANEN FORMER VICE PRESIDENT, HUMAN RESOURCES BED, BATH AND BEYOND, NEW YORK CITY

Unstoppable Power offers a refreshing and necessary perspective on successful leadership. Jay Kuhns walks the talk and takes readers through a leadership journey that shows us how to leverage and add value through energy, boldness, and relationships. Walk away feeling ever more ready to lead with confidence and be the "CEO of YOU" as Jay puts it!

LOTUS BUCKNER, CHIEF PEOPLE & CULTURE OFFICER, CHOWBUS, CHICAGO IL

UNLOCK THE UNSTOPPABLE POWER OF LEADERSHIP WITH JAY

Every now and then you meet someone who you feel you have known your whole life, a kindred spirit, a brother in arms. That's exactly the sensation I had when I first spoke with Jay. As we talked about people, engagement, and achieving success it was clear that our leadership thoughts were cut from the same cloth. Not born out of theoretical musings, but from our hands-on experiences of leading teams in difficult situations and leading them to success.

What I love most about Jay's leadership approach is its simplicity and how he makes it accessible to everyone from junior leaders to the CEO, which is an amazing skill, and shows his deep knowledge of leadership.

For anyone who has been part of a successful team and remembers what it felt like, Jay's key principles of *Energy, Risk Taking* and *Relationships* will resonate strongly.

I know from my own experiences that these are the key ingredients needed to create teams that know what's needed to succeed, and that have the confidence to achieve repeatable and sustainable success.

In the post-pandemic, fast changing, highly competitive, remote-working world that we will live in, many of the more traditional command and control leadership approaches, which never really worked, will struggle even more. And it will be those leaders that can embrace the Unstoppable Power approach to leadership that will be able to create high performing teams that will thrive and put them in demand as leaders.

As you read this book, many of the principles will feel familiar, and that's because much of leadership is common sense, but sadly that's not the same as common practice. What Jay has done is created a process whereby you can take these learnings and make them your own to elevate your leadership to the next level.

Lastly, of all the elements of Unstoppable Power, the one that lasts well beyond the adrenalin rush of achieving the goals is the relationships. There is a camaraderie that is forged in the heat of battle or when facing the toughest of challenges, and its these relationships that endure.

I recognize many of the qualities I admire in people with whom I have been successful, in Jay and I know that we have now embarked on a friendship that will last a lifetime.

Thank you, Jay, for sharing your experience and expertise, and providing a clear roadmap that will help create that next generation of great leaders.

Gordon Tredgold

INTRODUCTION

I flat out love what I do. Helping leaders find their way through difficult or highly complex workplace issues, supporting young leaders who have unlimited potential but don't have the mentor they need to move ahead rapidly, or supporting the executive who wants to break through to the next level of their career...paying it forward is not just a cliché for me...it's everything.

Hello, I'm Jay Kuhns. I help people become leaders and leaders to become unstoppable. Bold? Of course! No effective leader ever sat idly by waiting for the world to come to them and offer the chance to make a difference. The best of the best make it happen.

You can too.

Leading matters. In fact, without bold leadership in today's world all of those dedicated and hardworking employees will be done a massive disservice. I firmly believe 95% of all organizational problems are based on leadership. With leadership comes a tremendous responsibility that directly affects the lives of those you lead and those you serve.

I understand what it is to feel the weight of the world on my shoulders. I've served in executive roles for more than twenty years making decisions that impact tens, hundreds, and thousands of employees. Great leaders are essential and needed more than ever. Since you haven't closed the front cover (or swiped to another app if you're reading the eBook), I suspect you agree.

I want to introduce you to the three core elements that fast-tracked my career. They have been, and still are, the lynchpin to my success from my 20s to today, now 30 years later.

The first is ENERGY – you need to consistently bring energy to your role.

The second is RISK – don't be afraid to make tough decisions. My career has been one example after another of taking calculated risks that resulted in opportunities I never imagined could happen so quickly.

The third is RELATIONSHIPS – prioritize being known as the leader who literally shows they care about everyone. Arrogance is a credibility killer.

My hope in writing this book is to help you accelerate your career. For that to happen, I must ask you to partner with me as you go through this short read. I ask that you be willing to implement new ways of thinking about your leadership style. My goal is for you to have a fresh perspective on what you already have in you and make you more effective, regardless of your current role.

These pages contain concrete, actionable steps you can take – immediately – that will lay the foundation for massive growth and success. After many years of wanting to share my knowledge and having countless people ask me when I would write my book, wallah, here it is. Your part in our partnership is to go through it and embrace the three elements (Energy, Risks, and

Relationships) to become the leader you know deep down you can be.

I'm grateful you've trusted me thus far by picking up this book. I can promise you I condensed many years of experience in a format that is easy to consume. Think of this as just you and I at a coffee shop working through a leadership coaching session.

Let's go!

CHAPTER 1
THE WORLD OF WORK IS UPSIDE DOWN

THE BEST OR WORST OF TIMES?

I had two conversations recently with prominent Human Resources (HR) executives from large organizations, one in Pennsylvania and the other in Florida. I'm always looking at the positive in any situation, which means I don't get into too many complaint sessions; however, executives all over the country are faced with more challenges than ever so there's a little more noise in the system than usual...and these two had plenty to complain about.

More humans are walking this planet than ever. Yet, organizations from the behemoth national level companies with large, distributed workforces to mom-and-pop ice cream stands are all desperate for talent. To be more accurate, it's not that they can't find them; again, people are everywhere - it's that they can't retain their people, let alone engage them in a contemporary way as leaders.

The relationship between each executive and the CEO is absolutely critical, now more than ever before.

Organizations are investing millions of dollars to raise salaries, update technologies, improve working conditions, and implement creative ways to retain their people. Mind you, in most cases, this money wasn't budgeted. The balance of power in the employer-employee relationship is shifting. So employers are scrambling to find the right language, offer the right incentives, and create the right atmosphere to keep their talented workers. The bad news is – it's not working.

What do you say to your CEO when he or she exclaims: "We just invested forty million dollars into our people, but our turnover has not changed! What is our plan to resolve this?"

I'll say it again, you better hope you have established a relationship with the CEO, or it's your job on the line. The relationship between the executive team and CEO is so important. I never took an executive position unless I reported directly to the CEO.

Too bold? Perhaps, but effective.

Once, I was the finalist for a terrific role, but I would have reported to the COO. It was a non-negotiable for me, so I left the negotiating table. "I either report to the CEO or I simply can't take the position, the employee voice through the HR executive is too important to not have direct access to the CEO."

I don't know if the others on the executive team thought I was an arrogant jerk or problematic; I do know that a few days later, I got a call. Apparently, they did some reorganization, and my position, should I still want it, would report directly to the CEO. I took the job.

So here I am, many years later, still in HR, having these two different but similar conversations with other high-level executives, and they are scared to death. Many companies are experiencing a turnover rate north of 20%, and in some cases, much higher. Twenty percent! Fifty percent! Ouch! Let me put that into perspective. If you have 40,000 employees, consider the staggering number of hires you will need each year to simply keep up with a 25% turnover rate? Turnover at that level doesn't move your company culture or its profits forward at all. It doesn't even keep you at a standstill, treading water. Let's pretend you could actually hire the number of people you need in today's hyper-competitive market for talent. Are your leaders ready to onboard them effectively, support the current team, and build the new culture you must create today to keep up? It's a nightmare without effective leadership.

One of those HR executives I spoke with said, "I never expected conditions to get like this. **It's the worst time** to be an HR professional."

To you, dear reader, I want to clarify something very important – the problem they are facing is not an HR problem; it's a leadership problem. (Often in this book, although I reference HR, I'm also referring to leadership at all levels).

I look at today's employment environment differently. I think **it's the best time** to be a leader. If you are as passionate about leadership effectiveness as I am, this is what you live for. All eyes are now nervously watching you. It's Go Time – so Let's Go!

TRADITIONALISTS ARE DYING

There are three tired truths about the HR world.

1. HR executives are typically less respected members than other members of the leadership team, such as finance, operations, marketing, communications, and legal.
2. HR is a necessary evil, filled with well-intended professionals trapped in a world of compliance, fundamental HR operations, and risk-avoidance.
3. HR work is boring (to those outside of HR who don't understand it's true potential)

I don't see HR like that at all! Leading the Human Resources function (or any leadership role) holds unlimited potential to drive the People Strategy and create a culture where people would love to work and just as importantly, not want to leave! I'm tired of the excuse that HR doesn't have a "seat at the table." If your skillset is at the level the job requires, you wouldn't have to complain about furniture – the seat – you'll have earned the privilege for your voice to be heard.

The woman who said it's the worst time to be in HR is a trusted, brilliant friend. However, she admitted to me that she's a bit of a traditionalist. She doesn't use social media (I'm going to get a lot more into this in coming chapters) and makes sure to remain in the constructs of how a C-suite person is *supposed* to behave.

Traditionalists are dying. The world moves too fast. Information changes too quickly, and attention spans are shorter. A haze has blurred the lines of many things that were once black and white. Yet, many old-school executives and managers still use outdated terms and slogans, such as "Check out this Hot Job!" It reminds me of the over-the-top voice-over in a cheesy used car commercial talking about their "Super Sale Exxxtravaganzzzzaaa!"

When I served as the Vice President of Human Resources at Johns Hopkins / All Children's Hospital, I told my staff we were going to be the best Human Resources team in the country. Some of my skeptical team members tried to tell me there was no way to quantify that. "How can that even be measured?" I told them that I didn't care. That level of quality is what I expected of them, and that we had it in our power to make our employees value us. I wanted them to believe we could achieve it. I wanted us all, including me, to behave as if we were the best of the best.

I believed in our power as leaders to make a difference.

I routinely visited every department. It was intentional. I wouldn't bring a notebook because I didn't want anyone to walk by me and think I was looking for someone to write up. I'd go as a colleague with a smile and ask people how they were doing and genuinely engage in a human-to-human conversation. I'd throw on a hair net, go to the cafeteria line, and yell out, "Who wants to get in on this selfie with me?" I'd quickly get surrounded by five or six great people that were serving the food. I would post that picture on Instagram and Twitter and write: *I love my team! You should work here!* And add the requisite hash tags. Soon enough, strangers would ask, "How can I get a job there?" The servers would also comment and add fun emojis.

Too many executives are afraid of interacting like this with their employees. That level of thinking can bring down a company.

Where is your energy at work? In a conference room somewhere or when you add an exclamation point to an email?

Other industries such as retail, manufacturing, transportation, are suffering as well. CEOs with hundreds of locations across the country are looking to their leaders for answers. They need to bring their very best to solve the unique challenges each one of these organizations are facing.

There are bright young people with potential that get promoted to management in their early twenties. You know the type; they flood their social media with pictures of weekend fun and some-times a bit too risqué content. How are we going to connect with and support these young leaders?

The hospitality industry is in trouble as the turnover rate in hotels and restaurants is worse than ever. Fewer people want to take the dirtiest of jobs. If you follow me on social media, and I hope you will, you'll see that I post a lot of food from the great places I love to eat. Some people think I never eat at home! As a result of my *philanthropy* to restaurants, I've become friends with many people from the owners to the frontline staff behind the bar. They are good humans, some that I occasionally connect with outside of the restaurant. When we discuss business, workplace culture, and employee retention, they tell me it's about the managers. If the employees perceive they are treated well, they'll stay.

They will stay. This is what leaders struggle to grasp. It is within our power to make a difference.

DON'T UP-SCALE, UP-SKILL

The worst thing you can do is to "train" your leaders. You don't train people, you train dogs. An ineffective manager is the weakest link of any management team. These are the by-the-book risk-averse managers that trigger employee unrest in many forms. They are too afraid of looking bad in the eyes of their "superiors," so they answer employee questions with policy quotes or, worse, threats and harsh comments. When questioned, they respond with their training, not their hearts.

For the record, I have nothing against training, but when it's all said and done, training is nothing but behavioral modification. There's nothing sophisticated or intuitive about it. It's a stimulus that provokes an automated response. Unlike in sports, where muscle memory is helpful because your body reacts instinctively to the fast-changing ebbs and flows of a game, in management, thoroughly trained individuals react like Compliance Officers. Stop training your managers and up-skill them instead.

Instill the competence and confidence all of your leaders will need to manage a stressed-out team member that challenges them. We would expect our CEOs and people with fancy titles to be savvy and able to handle complex conversations whether it's one-on-one, in a boardroom, in a lunchroom, or with a microphone in front of them as they stare into television cameras. Sadly even some senior leaders struggle to be the savvy leaders their organizations need.

We need savvy leaders at all levels to fully differentiate our organizations.

Lazy managers need to be removed swiftly. Leveraging the Employee Ombudsman role (an employee advocate that was accessible to any employee regardless of role) I implemented, I was able to gather information in a radically different way than in the past. If a leader mistreated a team member (you would be surprised how frequently this happens) they were gone. Period.

It's our responsibility as leaders to act. That's what we're here for.

Proactive moves invariably raise the camaraderie across an organization. Suddenly those who never thought of having a management position raise their hand and start to believe they can make a difference just like you.

THE WORLD NEEDS LEADERS

We face the most bizarre times in the world of work. The younger generation is looking to belong. They want their lives to have meaning. But at this time in history, we don't have an event like the Vietnam War, where people marched on city streets or colleges. We don't have a great Martin Luther King Jr. leading a civil rights movement. So, the workforce wants to belong. They want to affiliate *with something*. The Baby Boomers are near the end of their careers. The union message is gaining momentum to meet that need for affiliation. Companies are faced with new remote work models and hybrid approaches to create a retention pathway all while trusting their employees to be as productive working from home.

But make no mistake about it – this is not a doom and gloom book. What I shared with you in this first chapter is a glimpse into the working/career world in our country. This book focuses on how to up-skill YOU so that you can stand out from the competition, lead your company to greatness, change lives for the better, including your own, and write your story with you as the hero.

Contained in this book you'll find answers I could not find anywhere else. Should you put these teachings into action, you will change the trajectory of your leadership career. I don't care if you're 25, 35 or 55 years old – if you still want to be better, time is on your side. Too many leaders don't know what to do, and don't know where to turn for help. Now there is a new option. Every company needs savvy leaders who aren't afraid to make bold decisions and lead form the heart. It's your time to be that leader.

I'm going to teach you to master my three major elements of leadership:

1. Energy
2. Risk
3. Relationships

They say knowledge is power. That's BS. It becomes a burden if the knowledgeable person is afraid to speak up or act. It is the manifestation of knowledge that demonstrates power. Eradicate limiting beliefs that have held you down. It's time to go to work. Grab a pen, notebook, iPad or highlighter and turn the page. Get ready to lead. Let's Go!

CHAPTER 2
YOU CAN NEVER THINK BIG ENOUGH

DEATH BY STAGNATION

Some of what I've discovered in my extensive leadership journey is when an organization falls into routines, it means they have figured out something that works for them. It can bring a particular flow and measure of consistency to the workplace. It feels good to work for a company with a sense of alignment, where the vision shared by the leadership team is accepted and executed. The problem, however, is this – although they don't realize it, those organizations slowly inch closer to the proverbial cliff where jagged rocks lay waiting below.

The strength and commonality of purpose, which evolves into a routine –(the way we do things here) –, can be exactly what makes organizations and leaders stagnate. At the same time, companies that aren't afraid to think and lead differently pass the stagnant one by. Every organization, big or small, must constantly prioritize innovation. Not a new concept, yet so many struggle to build this into their strategic plans. For those that embrace leadership innovation, the future is limitless. I'm not against great routines, I'm just saying what worked ten years ago or five years ago doesn't work as well today and certainly won't work as well in the future.

My question is this: if something works, is it okay to stop trying to improve it and, instead, fall into the trap of a corporate comfort zone? My favorite mantra is this: you can never think big enough! Those who implement new strategies and methodologies will eventually topple those who get to the top but are trapped doing the same things. The number one spot is not a reserved seat. It needs to be earned and won every month, every quarter, and every year.

I am an innovator. If you saw me, the Human Resources executive, with a t-shirt on, you'd see the many tattoos I proudly display from my shoulders to my wrists. I'm not typical. I don't look typical. I don't have typical energy. I don't love chatting about typical results. You shouldn't be either. Typical is for managers who play it safe and who never consider that they could move to the next step in their career. It's not that I want to, it's more that I feel forced, compelled even, to innovate my strategic leadership vision.

Whether it's a contemporary approach to talent acquisition, social media and digital strategies, employer brand, modern communications and engagement channels, labor readiness, developing an employee experience like no other, or most importantly, being an accessible executive...clinging to the status quo is absolutely unacceptable.

The last thing you want as a leader is for your great ideas to grow stale as you watch a competitor accelerate past you. I have repeatedly told my teams, "As soon as our competitors replicate what we're doing, we'll do something new."

Adopting the Never Think Big Enough philosophy is the fuel that powers innovation. It unleashes the spirit of collaboration and opens minds to engage with others, whether it is colleagues, clients, or the community. For this to work, the leader must check his or her ego at the door. Just because you're the one with the fancy title doesn't mean the idea needs to come from you. Your job is to foster a creative environment that will allow ideas to flow, then identify a great idea and gather everyone together to implement it.

Be mindful not to get intoxicated by your past success or get stuck on an ego-driven leadership style. If you're not constantly challenging yourself, you will lose. How would everything run if you grew by thirty percent? Is your perfect system built to scale, or will it only work with the current numbers? How does your system prepare the company to potentially be acquired? Never think big enough.

It may take a while for the impact to be felt but we all know of successful organizations that dominated their industries and ultimately whittled themselves down to the bone and out of existence. We all know companies once at the top of the food chain that don't exist anymore. Blockbuster is a great example of that. When Netflix, a small, fledgling streaming company approached Blockbuster for a partnership or to be acquired, Blockbuster turned them down. "Our customers don't stream movies."

Where are they now? Imagine if they had a leader who said, "Although our client base doesn't stream now, the Internet and technology overall is growing rapidly. How about we buy Netflix for pennies on the dollar and see how this plays out?

Think big and think big frequently. It doesn't matter who you are, whatever you're doing, whether you just started your own business, if you're a key employee, if you're at any management level, if you're the CEO, CFO or Chief Fun Officer, you can never think big enough! People love to follow visionaries. Play to win or suffer the consequences.

BIDDING WAR

The year was 1995; appropriately enough At the Gates' song *Blinded by Fear* was a hit on the heavy metal charts. On the silver screen Bruce Willis was back in *Die Hard with a Vengeance*, and an all-star cast powered *The Quick and the Dead* in a revisionist Western. As for me, I thought it was time to go for it and get that first formal leadership role.

Thinking big before I really understood what it meant.

I was working for a small human services agency, and although I enjoyed it, I needed more. I saw a position posted at a hospital 40 minutes from my house for a Manager of Training and Development in the human resources department and I applied. I had no experience and insufficient qualifications to get the job, which would be a recurring theme for me in my first few managerial positions. I got an interview and clearly remember stepping out of my car looking at the hospital and saying out loud, "This might be my new home!"

I was 28 years old and had one year left in graduate school. Conventional wisdom told me to wait until I finished my master's degree, but I shut that negative voice inside my head down. I was hungry. The interview went well. I drove home that night worried, not that I wouldn't get the job, but that I actually might.

I wrestled with dueling emotions: The first - I was about to conquer the world. The second – I'm about to fall off the professional cliff! However, the drive to succeed far outweighed any fear. I never liked playing it safe. It's boring. I'd much rather have a position that stretches me over one that bores me.

I was thrilled to get an offer from the hospital. I told my boss I was leaving and she congratulated me. An hour later, she called me into her office and made me a counteroffer to stay. I was caught off guard, to say the least. I left her office and rounded the corner, unsure if I should pump my fists in the air or pinch myself.

After a bizarre back and forth between employers in an unnerving bidding war of sorts, I was speaking with my boss when she smiled and leaned back in her chair, as if she saw the situation for what it was. "Jay, you need to take that job. You're ready. They see something in you that they need and you want to test yourself in a larger organization. I think it will work out great for the both of you."

The bidding was uncomfortable yet it validated my desire to get into management. Yes, I was unproven, not fully "schooled," and never had much work-related responsibility, yet, it showed me something about life – it will give you what you ask of it. You just need to be ready to make good on it.

I later saw this poem by Jessie Belle Rittenhouse, which summed it up much better than I could.

> "I bargained with Life for a penny,
> and Life would pay no more,
> However I begged at evening
> When I counted my scanty store;
> Life is a just employer.
> He gives you what you ask,
> But once you have set the wages,
> Why, you must bear the task.
> I worked for a menial's hire,
> Only to learn, dismayed,
> That any wage I had asked of Life,
> Life would have willingly paid"

To you, dear reader, I must ask – what have you asked out of life? What risks have you taken? When did you take your shot at a lofty goal? Or are you still on the sidelines, watching other people play at a high level, getting paid at a high level, living at a high level, while you stay where you are...comfortably safe?

My confidence and drive took me into a situation that I was unqualified for that ended in a bidding war. Leadership is not only your business life. You are the CEO of YOU. It's time to play the game at a high level, with great energy and take big risks that lead to big rewards. Why not think big? The career you want is possible if you believe - you can never think big enough!

CHAPTER 3
ENERGY AND YOUR PERSONAL BRAND

WHO'S THE GOAT (GREATEST OF ALL TIME)?

When I give keynote speeches, I often ask this question a few minutes in: "Who do you believe to be the most effective leader you've ever worked with or for?"

I can tell by the crowd's reaction that within six or seven seconds they've firmly placed the person they would choose in their minds. I ask a follow up question: What traits do they possess that makes them so effective? I ask the audience to shout out the traits that makes that person the number one leader to them.

"Visionary!"
"Compassionate!"
"Honest!"
"Integrity!"
"Passion!"

Many other traits bounce off the walls, thoughtfulness, work ethic, commitment, confidence, empathy, creativity, adaptability, accountability, positivity, risk-taking, and more. I allow the room to settle, each person is subconsciously trying to think of a trait not said yet.

Not surprisingly, no one says, "They are a whiz at excel!"

I continue, "Let's imagine that ten years from now, one of your employees is asked this same question...." I pause. I see some people wince at the thought of it, letting me think that they already feel embarrassed or don't believe there's any possible way one of their employees could mention them. I ask the question I feel some in the room were hoping I didn't ask, "What's to stop them from your name popping in their heads? You can make that happen, but first, you must learn how to manage your Personal Brand. Let's get started!"

To you, dear reader, who are in a leadership position or strive to be, I want to ask you the same thing. What's to stop your name from popping into the minds of those that work with or report to you? I'll answer that. You. Meaning that if we can do something with you and the way people think about you (your personal brand), you can be the greatest leader those you lead have ever known. I hope that excites you!

I, for one, want to be one of the most influential leaders my colleagues have ever known. It's not egotistical. I don't want a plaque, a statue, a gala dinner, or a parade. I want to serve others through my positive influence and thoughtful leadership style. I want people to smile at me when they turn the corner in a hallway and see me walking in their direction. I want people to know that they can come to my office or reach out via video, open up to me, and know that what is said will not only remain confidential, but more importantly, that I'll do whatever I can to support them. I'm here to help people. Aren't you?

To be an all-time great leader, I feel I need to build great leaders. I want to recruit them, up-skill them, inspire them, motivate them, and empower them. I want them to become the most remarkable leaders their team members have ever known. Can you imagine an organization with 800 leaders (managers or key-role employees) who all want to be the greatest leader of all time? What impact would they make? You would have the best organization ever! You'd have a half-percent turnover rate. You'd have brilliant people from all over the world begging to work for you.

That, my friend, is reimagining leadership. That, if put into practice, would be powerful, revolutionary even. But first, you must develop your personal brand to come anywhere remotely close to that. You have to become a vortex that draws in the best talent.

WHAT IS A PERSONAL BRAND?

First, let me explain what it's not. It's not a brand all about your personal life, nor is it all about your professional life. It's an intentional and intelligent blurring of the lines between who you are personally and professionally. You take snippets of many areas of your life, in blogs, pictures, videos, or even memes, and upload them to the major social media sites.

Your personal brand also reflects who you are in the workplace. It shows up in every office engagement, every meeting, and every hallway interaction.

Your personal brand precedes you wherever you go and lingers with people long after you've left. It's sometimes noted by how people talk to you, and more importantly, how they talk about you. If someone enters halfway into a conversation, people should figure out that it is you they are talking about because your traits are that well known. If you're in leadership, you must know this elementary truth; people will believe in you more if they believe in your personal brand.

You may think that you don't have a personal brand. After all, when most people think about branding, they think of logos, colors, a jingle, or maybe a slogan. They think of social media influencers in their fancy cars, colorful attire, even more colorful language, and millions of followers. You might think, *I'm just a team lead, manager, or executive – I don't have a personal brand. I can't. It can ruin my career or pigeonhole me. The brand that matters is the organizations, not mine. I don't want one, and I don't need one.*

Here's the truth – you already have one! People think of you a certain way when they hear your name, see your email come through, or speak with you. A personal brand is almost like karma; for those who believe in it, you give back what you give off. Let me be candid: if you are an uptight controlling manager that locks him or herself in the office, doesn't allow walk-ins, doesn't proactively round with employees and when you do it is only because you are forced, and all you ever feel comfortable discussing is work, work, work – that's your personal brand! You're boring. You are not inspiring anyone...and sadly, your credibility is gone. Sorry, but this needs to be said.

The good news is you can repair your personal brand, and I will show you how! A grave misunderstanding for those in leadership or those who aspire to is that we must always speak the company script, be company men and women, and never make waves. Let me tell you a secret, the executive team is not looking for management clones. They hired you, so be you! Tastefully, of course.

The first thing you need to do is figure out who you really are. What do you bring to your employees, clients, colleagues, and their families? What do you bring to your household? What are you passionate about?

For example, if you know every character's name in the HBO series, Game of Thrones – does anyone know that? Are you an avid sports fan? Like me, do you love the Tampa Bay Lightning?

Are you a fantastic cook? Do you spend hours researching recipes and then create masterpieces on a plate? Do you write reviews for recipe sites, travel sites, restaurants, or hotels? Do you attend church twice weekly and love God with all your heart, soul, and mind? Are you in a bowling league complete with your own shoes and ball and never score under a 200? Are you a history buff, a conspiracy theorist, an active political agent for your party, a sneaker-head, a tattoo junkie, a jazz lover, or a health nut? Why doesn't anyone in your office know?

I challenge you to do an honest reflection of who you are. You may determine that you're a quiet, thoughtful, I don't want to rock the boat type of leader. Cool. Now you know.

For me however, energy rules.

I'm almost always "on." I've been told I have energy for days, I'm tireless, and I'm a machine. What I give off is not fake, it's who I am. I'm not energetic because one day I decided to be, thinking I'd be a better leader - I've always been this way. I've seen fake enthusiastic people. They only turn on when in a meeting or on a stage. But when you walk into their office and they look up at you, they barely look away from their screen, don't get up from behind their desk, don't flash you a bright smile and tell you how nice it is to see you. The energy you give off has to have an end goal or else it's just a lot of arm flapping and loud talk.

I bring as much energy as I can. Energy inspires. It's contagious, and people feed off of it. The right energy attracts the right people. We all enjoy watching and listening to charismatic speakers/leaders, and we want to hear them or watch their YouTube videos because it sparks something that we can connect with. Energy is a medium for universal connection. When I'm at work, I give the same high energy when speaking with a janitor, a neurosurgeon, or the CEO.

You may say to yourself, *but I'm not like you, Jay. I'm an introvert.* To which I would say, "So what? Still, bring the energy! There were times in your life when you've been excited or enthusiastic. Don't let the label rob us from seeing what excites you and from allowing you to influence us with your knowledge and perspective. Be an introvert at home, and lead from the front at work! Consider what drains your energy and thoughtfully prepare to store that energy for when you know you'll need to use it. You don't have to be like me, just be your best, upbeat self whenever you can.

My energy is authentic. I often get invited to speak to groups and sometimes large crowds. I know some great speakers that give it all they have on the stage, but then are exhausted and need three hours to recoup. Their energy is left on the stage and they enter the Green Room or hotel room drained. And that's okay, but it is not me. Like them, I give it my all when I'm in front of a crowd, but my energy doesn't dissipate when the crowd goes away. On the contrary, my body keeps rolling with positive energy. I'd be ready to do it again. Take me to the next ballroom!

I've always had great energy. Ever since I was ten years old, probably before ADD was a known diagnosis, I had it. I think the difference is that once I realized I expressed my energy more than most, I doubled down on it. It felt good. I developed a craving for it. I love to be around other people. Exchanging words with someone, i.e., conversation, energy, wisdom, advice, or information, fuels and inspires me.

I coupled my energy with my graduate work and turned it into a fantastic career that has put me in rooms with everyone, from ultra-high achievers to kids getting out of high school just entering the workforce. My journey has been nothing short of a blessing.

My personal brand centers on who I am. I'm an executive-level leader, I'm into fitness, my faith, and I love humor – I usually express it more as self-deprecating than anything else. I take my work very seriously; I don't take myself too seriously. To all leaders reading this book, self-deprecating humor works. The last place you want to be is on anyone's pedestal; it's a long, painful fall. Even though you didn't ask people to put you there, they do so by default, either because of your title or accomplishments. Make fun of yourself from time to time. People love it, and it makes you far more accessible than your counterparts. I want to make sure you know that it's okay not to be viewed as Superman or Wonder Woman.

BLOG IT UP!

After several decades of working in major organizations, attending multiple leadership development programs, participating in strategic planning retreats, lunch and learns, and being a part of a small team that made decisions for thousands of employees, I decided to write a blog about leadership and what it means to me. At first, the ever-surprise-attacking fear called Imposter Syndrome hit me in the face. *Who do you think you are? It's not like you've been the CEO of these organizations. It's not like you're a Four Star General. You're not a household name. You're not even a professional writer! Yet, you want to start a blog? Who's going to read it? Oh my God, this is going to be so embarrassing for you.*

And on and on it went in my head... well, not for that long. I quickly told that fear to leave me alone. I didn't want to start a blog to feed my ego, my energy needed another form of release. I knew I'd gone through so many leadership experiences that others could learn from. Why wouldn't I want to share it?

I started my blog, No Excuses HR – Holding Ourselves Accountable, on a Monday. The date was October 18, 2010.

In that inaugural blog, I wrote:

I realize more and more how tired I am of hearing excuses for why things cannot be done.

I also appreciate more than ever when a team comes together.

How has it been for you? How have you overcome the challenges of leaders that have long ago lost the passion for their work? How have you created the energy in your teams to push and push until you get the results you need?

I'd love to hear from you.

No excuses.

It was a short blog, and it was received with a whopping three comments. I was pumped! Three people took time out of their day to comment on my first blog! More importantly, I kicked Imposter Syndrome in the teeth and set out to accomplish what I said I would do!

Recently, as of this writing, I wrote a blog entitled, Rattled. In it, I confessed that when I received one of my first major promotions and was now the final word on HR matters at my organization, I thought to myself, "I don't know what to do sometimes. What if everyone finds out?" In that blog, I mentioned one of humanity's biggest nemesis, Imposter Syndrome, and shared how I've been rattled many times over my life.

It has now been 12 years and the blog is going strong. Not strong in the sense that I've monetized it, but strong in that I love sharing my positive insights with the universe. I love it when I receive positive feedback or that someone needed to hear what I had to say. It's quite humbling actually. If I haven't blogged in a while, someone will mention it to me. I love when people respond or comment that they needed to read that. It has become a part of the very fabric of my brand.

I write about leadership, strategies, insights, failings, and personal struggles. As a leader, I offer a clear line of sight into my thoughts and emotions. I write when I'm happy and when I'm upset. What you get is who I am. When my organization struggles, when we experience a massive growth surge, or when there's a significant policy shift; I write about it.

One of the things I didn't expect from it, but I'm glad happened, is that it gave me clarity of my core beliefs. We often don't sit down to examine our feelings on different topics, but after blogging for more than a decade, I can read how I truly feel, giving me a better sense of myself. I often write about fear and how we need to overcome it.

I remember when the Johns Hopkins Health System acquired my organization. When I blogged about it, I didn't take it as a threat even though executive teams are often replaced following mergers or acquisitions. That's not the energy that flows through me. I wrote how our organization and my team could leverage this change. I wrote, "Let's get excited and go!"

I've been asked how do people define my brand, I say, "My brand is a combination of very high energy, a positive attitude, kindness, and probably a little more energy. I use the term, Fired Up, all the time. People often tease me about it, 'Jay, are you fired up today?"

My high energy brand is who I am.

Who are you? Find out, and then share it with the world. Tell Imposter Syndrome that you're no longer paying attention to the noise inside your head. We need you, the real you.

CHAPTER 4
RISK PART ONE

WHAT WOULD YOU HAVE TO DO TO LIVE THERE?

Several years ago, I was having a conversation with my youngest child. He was still in high school and we were enjoying the view and breeze from the balcony of my condo that overlooks the ocean. Recently, the scenery had changed somewhat. I still had a great view of the water, but the taller and more modern condo next door had completed some updates and clearly caught his attention.

My son looked at the building and said, "Dad, I love your place, but... what would you have to do in your career to live there?" He gazed upward and pointed to the penthouse on the 20th floor.

I didn't answer quickly. I stared at the windows of what I would imagine was an immaculate penthouse. I turned to him and said, "I would have to take more risks in my career to live there."

"What does that mean?" he asked. That question opened the door for a thoughtful conversation about career growth. We talked about risk and recklessness, including some of the riskier things I had done to rapidly climb in jobs and scope of authority. The conversation pivoted to one of a father advising his son to go out and get what he wants out of life. I told him not to wait for the perfect time to do something; those times rarely come.

I'm not a great waiter. Not in terms of a restaurant server, I mean it in the sense that if I can have something in five minutes, I don't like waiting six days for it. I never wanted to wait, wait, and wait for an opportunity to open up so I could advance my career. My plan did not involve waiting and grinding it out and receiving a 3% merit increase a year. To go from employee to team lead to supervisor to assistant manager to manager to district manager to assistant director to... nope. That is an excellent growth path for many, but not for me.

As soon as I got into business, I wanted to accelerate my career as rapidly as possible. That meant I had to soak up as much knowledge as I could from the brightest people around me as quickly as possible...and, to take as many risks as possible to move quickly.

Many wonderful people have worked for organizations for 15, 20, 30 years and more. Some call them "lifers," as if they've given up on their dreams and remained content with where they were. I never thought of them that way. In fact, I thought the opposite was true. I viewed them as people who were totally committed to the company. If that were the case, that would be the result of outstanding leadership, meaning that in some cases, the executives took such good care of these employees and their families that they were "all in" with the organization. In my opinion, you can tell there has been great management if the organization has "lifers."

I valued those employees at every position and company I worked at. I wanted to learn from previous mistakes that only they remembered. Those employees and managers were a massive repository of knowledge that I used to guide me around landmines I would have never known were there. I also leaned on them to help me make decisions to ensure I didn't repeat the failures of the organization's past. I knew that with their brain-power and my ambition, I could be a senior leader quicker, which was always my goal.

*Side Note: The word Ambition has taken a bad rap as of late. I love the word. This is what it means: a strong desire to do or to achieve something, typically requiring determination and hard work.

And 'suddenly' I was an executive. How did I get to that level so fast? It wasn't luck. It wasn't fate. It wasn't being in the right place at the right time. It wasn't that I put it up on a vision board and claimed it every morning. The number one reason I advanced so quickly in my career and jumped when most people took baby steps is this – Risk. I wasn't afraid of it. In fact, I embraced it. Looked for it. Craved it.

In a previous chapter, I shared my thoughts on energy and the importance of passion and playing all out. I had an energy that simply outmatched my competitors for the jobs I went after. I don't say it to brag but to authentically share with you that passion and energy and taking some risks can differentiate you; however, you must deliver when your desk lands in the big office. My energy and calculated risk-taking helped me over-come what might have been months of experience instead of years. It helped me overcome one form of formal leadership to another, which gave me the self-confidence to go after that breakthrough job.

I'm really comfortable in my own skin. I'm the same person and act like me regardless of what room I walk into. I was just never satisfied professionally being too comfortable in a particular role for too long. I always wanted more. In order to get it, I had to make sure I over-delivered and impressed the executive team while also learning to see the broader organization-wide view.

High levels of good energy attract and inspire people. That's the good news. The not-so-good news is that it also puts you in a position where you must deliver. I was never afraid I wouldn't deliver. Sure, I was worried that I was in over my head at times, but the fear of not performing at a high level never slowed me down. Just because I hadn't done something yet did not mean I couldn't do it. If I hadn't taken the risks, I never would have broken through so early in my career.

Moving into my first junior executive role reset the bar for the rest of my career. I was now seen in a different light. I was an executive. Now there were no limits. Now other organizations that had c-suite vacancies had me on their radar, and I leveraged that to take even bigger risks in more senior roles.

I had always felt drawn to highly influential leadership roles. My father was a very well-respected and influential United Methodist Minister. He served large churches and people always spoke highly and reverently towards him. I watched him effectively manage complex situations, sometimes terrible ones, and watched people in grief, anger, or sorrow put on a smile and thank him. I knew I wanted to do something like that. I wanted to be in a position where I too could be influential and serve others. I felt it was my destiny and I was willing to work hard to achieve it.

A core element of my success was always being willing to take the risks necessary to advance myself. I took risks in my late 20s that put me in a position to be where I wanted to be in my early 30s. Now that I'm in my 50s... nothing has changed! I still take risks because they continue to yield great results. Am I comfortable taking them? No. Is it scary? Yes. Do I feel pressure to deliver? Absolutely! I get an unbelievable rush from doing good work and making an impact. You can't be a change-maker and not be a risk-taker.

STOP CYA'ING!

Too many managers are in CYA (Cover Your A**) mode. They worry about their careers or potential political fallout at every turn instead of driving change, sticking to their guns, and leading the way. They think the mountain is too high, the effort required is more than they can spare, and they let misguided thoughts of failure paralyze them. Analysis paralysis is alive and well.

The truth is, the people who are supposed to follow you, want to follow you! They want to be led. They want to be inspired. But you have to give them a reason to follow you. When the naysayers mention something that sounds like they're against your plans, it's not them talking; it's their fear. Your job is not to cajole their unfound nervousness. You were brought in to cut through it and get the organization's people to a better place.

When you're in CYA mode, you make self-serving decisions. These are usually safe, calculated decisions. These decisions are dangerous because they jeopardize your position, limit your effectiveness, and erode your credibility.

Self-serving decisions are not meaningful or impactful, at least not in a good way. Breakthroughs happen when you stop trying to protect yourself and instead focus on serving the organization, even if your decisions are not popular at the time. That's when the powerful connection with the team happens. That's when the alignment becomes palpable. That's when the leadership magic happens.

That is risk. Get comfortable with it...for it will serve you well.

CHAPTER 5
RISK PART TWO - RISK VS. RECKLESS

ME? A CONSULTANT?

There's a fine line between taking a considerable risk and becoming reckless. I had a wonderful job as the Vice President of Human Resources at John's Hopkins All Children's Hospital. I loved it there. Sure the monetary compensation was excellent, but the impact I was able to provide to that organization and their appreciation for me made it very comfortable, like home, which is a great compliment to the great colleagues I worked with there. All my friends and the people who knew me well knew I was very happy there. That was why many of them were in shock when they heard that I had resigned from my position and taken a consulting job with a national healthcare human resources strategy and recruitment process outsourcing firm.

My friends thought I was crazy and many texted me concerned: *Jay, you left JH? Is everything OK? Are you all right?*

It was their polite way of asking me, *What the hell were you thinking?!* Others applauded me and wished me Godspeed and good luck. They acknowledged that I had taken a big risk–stepping outside of my comfort zone. Those that questioned me and those that congratulated me were all stunned. They liked where they were, they had earned it, and it made them feel safe and comfortable. And that's okay if what you're looking for is some-place safe. I did the exact opposite of what they would have done. Many wouldn't have done it, but it was my decision, no one else's.

Many people have a skewed view about high-level consulting; you travel all over, eat far too highly priced meals, expense everything, and charge a ridiculous fee. Guess what? It's actually not true. I've been on many, many airplanes, stayed at many hotels, eaten at the same restaurants over and over and wondered if this was the glamorous life I had imagined? But what's not as commonly known is the amount of pressure to deliver that came with the new position I accepted. I wasn't scared or deterred though, after all, pressure is one of my favorite words, along with challenge, risk, reward, victory, and of course, energy.

It's easy to say you're not about the dollar when you've saved up a few. Still, I'll say it from a place of truth. I don't live for money, I don't jump to another role for the money, and I won't compromise my ethics, my word, or my reputation for it. While this new career put me on track to make more money, based on my performance, I felt I needed something else to fulfill me professionally.

This new job was a new mountain I had never climbed. Instead of helping just one great organization, I jumped into a position that could benefit multiple great organizations. The risk of leaving a safe place where I was loved and respected to go to a new organization as the "new guy" who never did the work before, panned out incredibly well. Leaving twenty years of hospital life for consulting seemed irrational to some, but it was just what I needed. It satiated the need for professional combat, to test myself, to find out how hard I could push myself. It amped up my always-high energy level. I was grooving and vibing to a new song. I was planning, strategizing, executing, traveling, delivering, interviewing…. Ahhhh I was alive!

The difference between risk and reckless is when you make decisions based on false data or from pure desire. Now, I love heavy metal music, in fact, true story, as of two weeks ago from this writing, I was at Jannus Live, a great venue for bands in St. Petersburg, FL. One of my favorite bands was tearing it up on stage; and without hesitation.

I hurled my fifty-five year old, high-level executive self into the swirling mosh pit. It went exactly as I figured it would as I left with a few bruises. My ribs were so sore that my workout with my personal trainer the next day was a bit rough. I have to tell you - it was exhilarating! I loved it and will happily do it again when the next metal band is in town.

That though, is not reckless. While it can get a little wild, it's not reckless. I've been in the center of so many mosh pits that I can mitigate serious damage, most of the time. When I go skydiving or scuba diving, it's also not reckless. It's one good old-fashioned heart-pounding, fear-killing, I-love-being-alive moment after another!

Reckless, for me, would be to take my love and passion for heavy music and leave my position to start a metal band. Leveraging my executive experience to move from a corporate role to a consulting role is one thing. Singing in dive bars for a living is something entirely different.

And while I love to bring that energy into all aspects of my life, how I apply that energy is something that needs to be managed. I say this to you to stress that as you read parts of what made me successful, in terms of taking a job I had never done – it was still a calculated risk based on many years of previous wins. I'm an average karaoke singer at best, and that depends how late into the night you hear me. It would be reckless to leave everything I've built just for desire and nothing else.

NON-NEGOTIABLES

While I don't shy away from risks, I prefer to run to them. There are things I won't risk, very few, but still, I do have some "non-negotiables." I would never risk my kids, family, grandchildren, etc. I would not risk my relationships with them. Not for fame, fortune, or all the free tattoos from the best artists. I won't risk my values either. I am as inclusive as it gets and no one and no situation will make me forego that. I won't risk my faith. I love my God and my church. Nor would I risk the organizations I have ever worked for. Not just my current employer, all of them. Risking any of these would be foolish and reckless. Now, my career? Pshh, that's another story!

It's a shame that countless numbers of talented people will never find true professional satisfaction in their lifetimes because they are too afraid of taking that all-important risk. They sit next to me in a café at another table complaining that they don't have enough of this or that. It takes everything in my power not to interrupt their conversation and ask, "So what are you going to do about it?" But I can't because polite society say's I'd be rude, and they would take it that way and not in the helping way I would intend.

Instead, I leave there, willing to bet 99 out of 100 times they will be saying the same complaints five years later. That, my friend, is sad. In order to break through, you need to take risks, leave the beaten path from time to time, trust your heart, unleash your creativity, and flex for the whole world to see your strength.

Now is your time. Take the risk, now. Don't wait. Do not justify your fear with a "practical" voice in your head. Practical voices don't win. Be the risk taker that makes all the difference.

CHAPTER 6
RELATIONSHIPS PART ONE

RELATIONSHIPS ARE CRUCIAL

There is nothing, and I mean nothing, more important in our lives than our relationships. A millionaire without good relationships is miserable, and a poor person with great relationships feels like royalty (albeit under financial pressure). Hearing someone say, "I love you," before you even say it, is a level of acceptance that every human being on the planet craves. It's neither a want nor a whim; it is a core, raw desire that comes from the depths of our very souls.

Your ability to manage human connections is the single best or worst trait you can have in this life. Being wanted, needed, and loved is so vital that the absolute worst criminals in the world get punished by isolating them away from other humans.

Relationships also provide a barometer as to whether you're living a good life or a bad one. If you're an adult and don't have any good friends of more than at least five years, there's a good chance your social skills are woefully lacking. The quality of relationships you have also indicates to the rest of us the type of person you are. If you hang out with people who are always trying to work the system, pull off some sort of scam, or do anything to get ahead, you're probably a pretty big jerk. On the other hand, if your friends are successful, loyal, trusting, hard-working, law-abiding, and kind, there's a good chance you're a pretty decent human.

To me, at the end of it all, the only thing that matters is my relationships. I protect and covet my closest ones with all that I have. My relationships determine how I'm treated, how I'm talked about, and how I'll be remembered. I'm referring to relationships in general, both personal and professional. But for the sake of this book and the context I hope you glean something from, I'm going to teach on the professional aspect of building bulletproof relationships that will accelerate your career.

Relationships are crucial to a good working environment and elevating your career as a leader. Crucial. At the end of the day, every workplace has an expectation, whether it's a hospital, a tech company, a marketing agency, a major grocery store, or a fast-food restaurant. That expectation is that we will work collaboratively, in synch, in harmony, and productively. We are all getting paid to perform a specific role that helps our organizations generate profit and add value.

Unfortunately, the human element comes into play and not everyone does what they are supposed to do, and not everyone behaves the way they're supposed to, which, if you think about it, is why there's a need for managers and leaders. There has never been a time when the business world needs leaders who understand how to not only manage but optimize people's talents as well. It is more imperative than ever to display savvy leadership skills.

I've worked with people with fancy titles, who received great paychecks, got awarded nice accolades, who happily sat behind their desks sleeping on their posts. Guess what? That doesn't work. Real people have real issues that require other real people to address them personally. World-class organizations are thirsty for high-energy leaders willing to take appropriate risks and build internal relationships that strengthen the fabric of the company. I sincerely desire that this book creates a fire in you so strong, that you visualize how impactful you can truly be.

Your title will give you the authority specified therein, meaning, if you manage twenty people, you manage twenty people. However, your relationships will determine how well you actually manage those twenty people. Regardless of how many subordinates you have under you in the org chart, it behooves you to put in the work to build trusting relationships with them now. Everyone matters; however, the key, influential people of the group are essential in order to move your ideas forward. You can have a great strategic plan, but if you're the only one trying to get it adopted by the masses, you're in for long, challenging days. Who wants that life? Who wants to go home or hang out with their buddies and brag about how ineffective they are and how it's everyone else's fault? Not me, and I would wager, not you either.

TWO THINGS I'VE DONE

The First:

In several organizations I've been privileged to work at, I made the decision to have a standing meeting with an executive-level peer once a month. You might think, *Oh, no, is this your advice for me? More meetings? Come on, man!* But hold on; you might be focusing on the wrong thing. Let me explain.

I focused on the very important strategy of building a personal relationship with each of my peers on the executive team. I would set it for an hour and would not break it unless it was totally out of my hands, which meant, come hell or high water, we were having this meeting. Sometimes we would spend the entire time on business matters, which was fine because it was highly productive.

Other times, though, not too often but often enough, the business matters would be squared away and there would be time remaining from the allotted 60 minutes. I would not end the meeting early. No, no, no, dear reader, that would be a terrible waste of the company's time! That's when I would ask about their health, spouse, children, hobbies, etc. As time passed, I knew their spouses and children's names by heart. Something happens in a human being when another person asks about your son Timmy's baseball game or how your spouse's business conference in Vegas went. An affinity, a personal attachment, connects two colleagues into, dare we say, almost friends or maybe actually friends.

I did this by design because inevitably, the proverbial shit is going to hit the fan. Something is going to go haywire, or someone is going to make a mess of things. You can count on it. When that happens, and the executive team is trying to best manage or mitigate an issue; that foundation of friendship, or at the very least likability or mutual respect makes it easier to take out any emotion and not attack each other. Instead, the issue on the table is tackled, not the other person.

That's what the organization expects you to do. However, sadly, the organization doesn't always get what it expects. It gets frazzled "leaders" first trying to assign blame on someone in the room and yada, yada, yada, everyone gets pissed and nothing gets fixed.

The workplace culture is a collection of many micro cultures that get mixed into a level of consistency. This is true in organizations with thousands of employees as well as in the inner dynamics of a small, five-person executive team. The level of trust, caring, and professional courtesy that comes from establishing the right relationships is powerful and long lasting.

I took the same mindset into my professional ecosystem. What came out was a level of trust, caring, and professional courtesy that enhanced our lives.

The Second:

In many positions I've held, other leaders reported directly to me. I'll refer to them as Direct Reports. One day, as they walked into a regularly scheduled meeting, I surprised them by having someone there with me. It was a woman who served in a senior role in the organization, and who, like me, people felt they could trust. I know I certainly did.

I informed my team of that day's meeting agenda. "We are not going to have our regular meeting today, instead, I have asked this special person to facilitate a feedback session on my performance."

My Direct Reports seemed caught off guard, just like I wanted them to be. "I'm going to leave in just a moment and when I do, she will ask three questions I want you to be at full liberty to answer honestly. The questions are, what should Jay do more of? What should Jay do less of? And what should Jay keep doing at the same level?"

Someone remarked, "Geez, Jay, I wish you had given me a heads up. I would have planned my answers."

I replied, "That's exactly why I didn't. I don't want anyone to feel the need to protect me or to tailor a vague answer for fear of repercussion or answers that are too politically correct. Please give her your honest assessment. She will collect the data and synthesize it into a document she and I will review. My goal is to serve you as best as I can. No one will get in trouble, she will not present her findings to my boss the CEO, and she will protect your anonymity and not tell me who said what." After that, I walked out, whistling.

Before the meeting, I had written a blog post about what I planned on doing on my leadership blog NoExcusesHR.com. When I walked back into my office, leaving them in another room to talk about me, I pressed the PUBLISH button, putting the blog out for the world to see what I was doing in real-time.

I feel the need to remind someone reading this, a very well known but seldom practiced truth – we are adults and, as such, have the ability to modify our behaviors. I did not doubt that whatever came from the meeting would come from a place of friendship and probably loyalty. So, I knew I could change what was necessary to make our group stronger, after all, I had told my team I wanted the best team in the country. I told them that when it was all said and done, I would do what it took for them to say I was the best leader they ever worked for, and I meant it.

When I met with the woman who facilitated the meeting, I was happy to know that it was not lost on them how much I believed in them and the trust I felt. I had built a solid foundation with each of them, and they saw me putting our relationships into action. "Jay, if you had their trust before, they'd probably write it out in blood for you now."

She walked me through the feedback, and I made a concerted effort not to give excuses for any perceived slights. Then, I met with the group of five and debriefed the topics they brought up. One of the more prominent things was that they needed more of my time. Prior to this feedback session I had made a huge effort to be very responsive to all of the organization's managers, department heads, and executive team that I wasn't available enough for my Direct Reports. I immediately modified my schedule-to include each of them weekly.

A second category of feedback was for me to participate more in their events, whether a team building, taco-Tuesday-type get together or even a personal one. I told them that I'd be honored to, but I also had to set the right tone. "I'll likely show up a little late and leave early. I don't want to blur the lines of our relationship." With the stage properly set, I would show up to things late and leave early, but when I was there, I was there, fully present and with great energy.

Side Note:

As a leader, you must keep the main thing the main thing, which is to ensure that those under you can always perform their duties effectively. And while you may not have trouble being overly friendly and personable with people and yet, stay in character at work, not everyone else can do so. There will always be some immature or extremely eager employees that will try to get lazy due to what they perceive to be a budding friendship with someone "high up." So, get in late, get out early, and keep the boat flowing, not rocking.

Just because I set specific time aside for the others on the executive team, managers, and my Direct Reports, did not mean I didn't need the positive respect of the people, not born from fear, but because they knew I genuinely cared about everyone. When you're the Vice President of Human Resources, and your organization employs thousands, you take it seriously, or at least, I did. My job was to champion our employees. I had to make sure they got what they deserved, not only in terms of compensation and a good work environment, but also when unfair issues arose, and a strong executive intervention was necessary. I was never afraid to move unfair or worse, harsh leaders out of the company.

I made it a required practice to walk the halls and meet the employees, as I have mentioned before. But in an organization of hundreds or thousands, they may all know you but there's no way you can know all of them, especially if you're not authentic in wanting to get to know them. Once a month, I'd be in different departments. Everyone is my colleague and should feel that way, but the only way to do that was for me to make them feel that way.

It was and is essential for me to create the impression that I'm an accessible executive who doesn't take himself too seriously. Even though they are performing life and death work, literally, at a hospital, it doesn't mean we can't have a good time doing it or enjoy the workplace.

As I would "make my rounds," I'd often whistle. Answer this question for me; yes, you, dear reader, you, please answer this question for me:

> *What would you think of a person that whistles*
> *as he or she walks toward you?*

If I can play mind reader for a moment, my guess is that you answered that the person is in a good mood and/or happy. Was I right? Nailed it! That is exactly what I wanted them to think when they saw me. That went right into my Personal Brand. "Here comes Jay. That guy is always happy, look at him whistling at work!" No one whistles when they're upset or sad. I forced myself to hard wire whistling into my Personal Brand. Well, to be candid, I didn't have to force myself too hard, it's not as if I had to stretch myself. It came naturally. But my point is I did it intentionally. Before people talked to me, I made sure they felt my mood – positive and happy. That, dear friend, is contagious. Who wouldn't want to work for that leader?

There was a time when I worked for someone who was the opposite of a guy that would whistle down the halls. It was early in my executive career and the culprit was none other than the CEO. Boy, was he moody! The executive team and managers would check with each other, "What type of mood is he in today?"

If he were in a good mood, he'd literally have a line of executives waiting to talk to him. If you got into that line early, you were safe, but if you were at the end of the line, chances were his mood was going to change and, being that you had already scheduled time with him, you were in for a rough meeting. His office would look like a ghost town when he was not in a good mood. No one would walk in, no one would be waiting in the seating area outside of his office, and heck, hardly anyone would even walk in the hallway near his office. As a 32-year-old newly minted executive, I swore that I would never be that type of person. I vowed always to be available and accessible and that it was up to me to create a connection with the employees, even if I didn't know them all.

How about you? What type of leader do you vow to be?

What do you want people to say about your leadership style?

And most importantly, how important are the relationships you have with everyone in your organization?

CHAPTER 7
RELATIONSHIPS PART TWO

BE INTENTIONAL

Read this closely; it is 100% in your power to have people who work for you, say whatever you want them to say about you. Just be intentional. I would walk quickly everywhere, not because I was in a hurry, but because I was excited to get to where I was going – there's a difference.

"A pep in his step" – that's one of the things I wanted people to say about me.

"A visible energy." – another thing.

Investing time with as many people as is reasonably possible, meaning, without compromising or neglecting other duties, will enhance your career. A person known for doing great work and that values his/her bosses and employees is a person with a great reputation. As a leader, I don't think there's a better compliment than when people say they trust you. Newsflash: good and bad news travels fast in the workplace. Also, leaders get talked about all of the time. Just as you talk about your boss, the people under you talk about you. What do you want them to say?

Side Note for newly promoted managers:

Oftentimes, high-performing employees that never had an itch to manage get promoted to a leadership role – a supervisor, manager, director, whatever. But what I'm saying here probably has more to do at the supervisor level. This may come across as harsh but believe me, it comes with your best interest in mind:

You've been working shoulder to shoulder as one of the team for a long time. However, you've been promoted and are now assisting with or are fully responsible for your former peer's performance appraisal. You are no longer equals in the work-place. These are people you've probably gone to birthday parties, weddings, Thursday night after-work happy hours, or may have had a bender or two on weekends. I say this respectfully but directly, without flinching; those relationships have to be over with, at the very least, curtailed.

Now, before you deem me a monster and a look of horror takes over your face, let me continue. On the flip side, there are new leadership peers you'll be working shoulder to shoulder with (even if now you have your own office) who are there to support you and bond with you as you progress in your career.

I use this strong language with you for two reasons:

1. I want to help you avoid getting into awkward situations that could cost you your hard-earned promotion.
2. As I always say, "You can never think big enough." Now that you have the attention of senior managers or executives, I want you to think bigger about your career. Today it could be one call center, but if you play your cards right, you could manage six call centers in three years.

I say this to first-time managers because that's the best time to teach them. If someone's goal is to make it to an executive leadership role when they turn 40, they can't start thinking like one when they're 39.

There are many layers to building great relationships but no two traits are required more than being authentic and being accessible. For example, I've been told countless times by frontline staff when they ask to meet with me privately, "Jay, I need to make more money."

I answer them, "Do you plan on being alive in three years?"

They answer, "Of course!"

I smile, yet very seriously tell them, "I can't simply give you more money. However, it is within my power to provide tuition support for you to go to school for a few years so you can earn the credentials required to get a higher paying job here. Let me help you, but this is a two-way street.

You see friends, a simple tuition reimbursement conversation is predicated on my accessibility to meet with a front-line entry-level employee; and my sincere desire to show my authentic self. I needed every team member to feel like I genuinely cared about them. And honestly, I did.

THE CHOICE IS YOURS

Building strong relationships is more than merely checking off a list of to-dos, smiling, being nice, and appearing to listen. Those are all well and good, but you must do those things authentically and take action for them to manifest into strong relationships. Absent authenticity, you're acting. No leader can act their way through eight to ten hours a day, five or six times a week, for a period of years. The phonies are always found out.

I recently received a personal note from a director of talent acquisition that worked for me many years ago. She reiterated how grateful she was that I put her in a position before she was completely ready and took the time to ensure her success. Even though I was present and supportive, I let her develop her own management style and way of doing things. She shared that her latest role was with a global company and was something she never dreamed would come about for her.

Her actual message was to say she spoke highly of me when giving her first remarks to the new team. Her message sounded so like her; graceful and classy. She said, "I did my best Jay impression, brought out my energy, and talked about risks and the relationships I expected to have with them." To say I didn't have a lump in my throat would be an outright lie. Stuff like that, my friend, proves a leadership life lived well.

At the end of the day, serving people authentically is the best way to become valuable, whether at work, at a social club, at a church, or wherever your feet take you.

Make the decision to prioritize relationships as a core element of your leadership style; not just with your peers, but with everyone. Is that a tall order? Of course, it is. Did you think life would get easier as you moved up the ladder? Embracing the power of relationships will transform your leadership journey. I guarantee it.

CHAPTER 8
MORE THAN JUST PERSONALITY

WAS THAT A COMPLIMENT?

I don't mind giving compliments. If you look great, I'll tell you, if you gave an amazing speech, I'll tell you, if you went above and beyond at work, I'll let you know. Compliments are empowering, not only for the receiver, but it also makes the giver feel good. Many years ago, author Gary Chapman came out with a groundbreaking book on relationships called, The Five Love Languages. Compliments are such vital bits of information to receive that – Words of Affirmation – are one of the five love languages. We love to be complimented!

As with most things, not everyone is good at everything all of the time. When it comes to compliments I've given, I cringe when I recall compliments that could have been construed as offensive. According to Dictionary.com, a left-handed compliment is a compliment with two meanings, one of which is unflattering to the receiver. Before I continue, I apologize if I have ever given you a compliment that praised you on one side and slapped you on the other.

In this short chapter, I will discuss an offensive compliment people have given me throughout my career. Enough people have said it, so I don't take it personally when I hear it now, but it doesn't change the fact that the compliment is not very complimentary.

Here it is: *Jay, your personality is an excellent fit for your job.*

To be fair to those who have said this to me, they often follow up with, *because you have a fantastic personality* or something genuinely kind. While I appreciate that they see how I embrace my role and feel it to be a natural fit for who they think I am; I did not become successful solely based on my personality. I've had my personality for as long as I can remember. Suggesting it is why I'm successful negates the years of school I put myself through, the lessons I've learned on the job, and the most critical elements to my success: understanding the power of energy, risk, and relationships. It's almost an insult to hear someone say your personality is what makes you successful when you've worked so hard for so long.

Whether or not you're a born leader has no bearing on the context of this chapter, or this book, for that matter. What makes you a leader is where you place your focus and your consistent approach; being kind, accessible, a listener, following through, supporting your colleagues and team members – all of that far outweighs some imaginary gift you might be born with. If you can light up the room with a joke on the spot or quietly and confidently carry yourself, you are intentionally making an impact. Leading is done from the front. No one will ever describe the best leader they ever worked for by how effectively they developed the annual budget.

Refrain from letting other people's descriptions of your personality determine your success or put a ceiling on your potential. This goes for introverts and extroverts: embrace the three elements to success – Energy, Risk, and Relationships. Do it authentically. Don't allow the self-talk machine in your head to convince you to play it safe. Be fully present at every meeting, don't be afraid to try something new, and make sure to take the time to nurture new and existing relationships. That has nothing to do with personality. That is all about deciding to lead effectively.

You are in proximity of people you can influence – direct reports, peers, and those higher up on the org chart – be your authentic self and you will positively impact them in ways that could open doors you have never imagined. Like a large stone dropped in a serene lake, what you say and do will have ripple effects far greater than just where the stone landed. The higher up in the organization you climb, the greater visibility you have, and people have of you, so make sure to be self-aware and be yourself. That and the three pillars will take you much further than your personality alone.

That being said, a good personality helps!

CHAPTER 9
SAVVY LEADERSHIP

BEING SAVVY

Being savvy means having an uncanny perception of people's personalities and egos and understanding how to navigate through all of that...stuff. At times, this leader needs to be silent and let the other person let out what's troubling them. Give them the space and time to have an energy burn, like a boxer who swings wildly with all of his or her might for a little while. The savvy leader will let them punch themselves out. Once the opponent is exhausted, they regain control of the situation.

Another key element to being a savvy leader is the ability to read a room. This is not a new concept, but for some reason, it seems to be overlooked by many in leadership positions. I've seen it mishandled countless times, so often that I'm writing about it so you can learn the dos and don'ts and propel your career forward at a much faster rate.

There have been many times I've walked into a meeting knowing I had the perfect solution. However, the solution gets misconstrued if the people who need to hear it feel unheard. A savvy leader will often hear the other team members out, ad nauseam sometimes, so they can gain the buy-in necessary to move forward. Earning the right to speak by listening to direct reports carries more weight than speaking because the title gives you the right. It also makes you far more effective and much more respected.

I'm not sure why people are oblivious to the mood and atmosphere of a room, whether it's a small, intimate meeting or a festive corporate function. I think it's a combination of hubris, not being self-aware, or not caring what other people think; regardless of the *why*, the results can be less than favorable, if not disastrous and almost always erode the leader's credibility.

I've been to countless conferences and even more meetings large and small and have learned there is an art form on how to communicate. I'm not going to pivot and expand into teaching you how to speak from the stage, perhaps that'll be my next book. However, I do want to point out some things that will immediately help you be more effective when speaking in any setting.

You need to understand how your message is coming across in the moment. This is an absolutely essential component of savvy leadership. Note the many variables in play simultaneously: are people smiling at you, nodding in agreement, smiling at each other, or giving you their full attention? Is there little movement in the room, are people making eye contact with you, taking notes, facing you, or interacting with you?

You, my friend, have the room when they are fully connected, engaged, and have effectively shifted and modified what you say and how you say it as the meeting has moved along. This is not easy. Making adjustments in real time is difficult. Without this skill however, you will never be able to fully unleash the power of energy, risk, and relationships. All eyes are on you and it's time to deliver.

Sadly, I've seen people in similar situations struggle mightily. There is too much commotion in the room, no eye contact, loud sighs, and people are on their phones or checking their watches – yet the leader speaking thinks he or she is killing it. Let me say this, it can happen to anyone. The savvy part comes into play when you recognize it and have the ability to pivot.

When I feel I don't have the room, I'll pause – this makes people who weren't paying attention look up at me – and then I say, "I don't get the sense my message is getting across the way I want it to, let me rephrase..." This technique gives me, and the others in the room, a much-needed redo.

Or, I'll ask, "Does that make sense? Someone, please give me some feedback with what you're hearing?" You have to understand that people do not always receive the message you believe you're sending. This technique initiates engagement and provides the way for clarity and discussion. It also allows you to take control of your message once more.

Pausing to ensure you are connected with the group takes a measure of self-confidence and humility. It also humanizes you as a leader that demonstrates how much you care not only about the message, but the people in the room as well.

BUT HOW?

So, the question you may have is how do I read a room? Great question! First, let's put reading the room in its proper perspective. It's not all about speaking or convincing others to buy-in to your ideas. Reading the room begins with how you walk through the door.

It starts with you and how comfortable you feel in your own skin. If you don't know anyone and realize everyone is dressed a little different, or you look over or under dressed, don't let the self-talk machine make you think people are looking down at you. Like most people, they are interested in how others perceive them, not what you're wearing! Walk in confidently knowing you deserve to be there.

Make eye contact galore. Nothing equates to confidence than looking people in the eyes, not a strut, not an outfit, and certainly not a title. If you're looking at your shoes or examining the signage, you look uncomfortable whether you are or not. If you're in a meeting, look at who's speaking. If you're walking through a crowded office party, don't look down, look at anyone who glances your way and smile. If you do that, don't be surprised if total strangers come up to you and ask you where they met you before. Eye contact and a smile are wonderful icebreakers.

Be your expressive self. If you're with four other people, you being the fifth, and the tone is monotonous and "professional," don't be afraid to speak with enthusiasm when it's your turn. Hell, you should speak with enthusiasm all the time. Remember: energy!

Reading the room means knowing when to liven up a dull or slow meeting. I was in Detroit with a client working through several complicated issues. Two hours into the meeting I was still in high gear.

"This is great, Tom. Really valuable insight. I'm sure we can make this happen!" I said.

One of the executives chuckled and said, "Jay, you should have your own morning show!"

We went down that rabbit trail, of what my morning show would look like, for several minutes, and when we resumed to the matter at hand we were still in high gear because I was still in high gear. Reading the room is not just watching it, it's having the ability to make a sustained impact.

Not every leader is an effective communicator. There. I said it. Many people get promoted for being high achievers or their technical expertise, not so much for their people skills. If you're in a position to hire a supervisor or manager, understand this important fact: the first competency to look for should be how well he or she communicates.

UNDERSTAND HOW YOUR COMPANY GENERATES REVENUE

Another competency of a savvy leader, particularly for HR executives although I submit it applies to every manager; is to understand how your company makes money. This is different than knowing the process of creating the widgets and how much they sell, but how the company actually makes money. Without that knowledge, you'll never become a respected member of the leadership team.

You may know all there is to know about how to do your work whether it's at the Boys and Girls Club, Apple, Johns Hopkins, the local grocery store; or fully understand the ins and outs of the most efficient way to complete your daily tasks. However, if you don't understand how the impact of proper bedside etiquette, retail store operations, recruitment tech stacks, financial services, insurance reimbursement rates, or the supply chain impact on how your organization generates revenue your credibility as a leader will crash and burn.

A HIGH STAKES STORY

Years ago, I was involved in an internal search for a high-level position – the Special Assistant to the CEO for the entire health system. As far as assistant positions went, this was the crème de la crème. I wasn't in an executive role at the time; I was a middle manager, so I had plenty of people to answer to if I chose the wrong slate of finalist candidates, so my team and I went through an extensive process just to identify suitable employees for the position. One particular candidate had a great relationship with the CEO, which turned out to be her downfall, and nearly mine.

To her dismay and surprise, as well as others who were in the know, I eliminated her from the pool of finalists. She was a manager in the organization, was very good at what she did; had a stellar resume, was well-liked, was qualified for the position, and, as I stated earlier, had a great relationship with the CEO. Many were surprised that she didn't make the final round, and as you might suspect, she was bitterly upset with me.

The CEO actually called and asked me to explain why she didn't make it to the final round. I calmly explained the thorough interview process, her lack of attention to any details, and how she clearly did not take the process seriously based on her assumption that she was going to get the job. I explained that she was so ill prepared for my questions that it was embarrassing.

I believe my heart rate was just around 200 beats per minute at this point during the call.

My explanation was good enough for him and he thanked me for conducting the search so professionally. She, however, was pissed.

I decided to schedule a meeting to speak with her about why I made the decision I did, and I scheduled it in her office. (*I wanted her to feel comfortable, empowered even. Had I scheduled the meeting in my office, it could have come across as a power play on my part.*)

The office was chilly, not in temperature but in how she greeted me. It was more of a slight tight-lipped nod instead of a welcoming hello. The room may have been an icebox. She is considerably shorter than me, so I immediately sat down. (*I* *wanted to shift the perspective of me standing over her). After a brief hesitation, she too, sat down.

I began, "Before we start, I came here with two goals for our time together. First, I will answer your questions honestly about the process and final decision. Secondly, I want you and I to continue to have a good working relationship when I leave."

She was stunned into silence. The office gossip machine had reached my ears of her displeasure with me so, perhaps, she was expecting me to come in there and try to put her in her place or argue with her. It certainly seemed that she was ready to complain and blame. However, she could only nod affirmatively at my two goals, albeit still tight-lipped.

"Would it be okay if I start, or would you like to go first?" I asked. (I didn't just start explaining myself, I gave her the option/control of who started the conversation).

"Go ahead," she said, which were the first words she had uttered since I entered her office.

I explained not only the process but also the reasoning behind why the process was the way it was. I let her know what we were looking for, how we were making assessments, and the difficulty in finding one candidate from a pool of qualified candidates. Then I told her what the finalists had said and done. I didn't have to compare what they did to what she did, I wasn't trying to win an argument, I was matter-of-factly presenting the facts from my end. She could not have had any idea of how well the other candidates prepared themselves, and was clearly now realizing how poorly she managed herself in the process. I gave a very comprehensive picture of the entire process. *(I made sure not to make it personal and tell her what she didn't do or could have done better. That allowed her to take my information in without anger or causing a rebuttal).*

At the end of our meeting, she was blown away by what her competition did and admitted that she had taken the interview process for granted due to her strong relationship with the CEO. I never received a Christmas card from her but nor did I get a box of coal sent to my office. She was a manager of patient relationships in one of our hospitals, so we had to work together when an issue about patient care arose. Thankfully, when we worked together, we did so amicably and efficiently.

I did not give her a free pass, meaning that her complaints about me had reached my ears and it was the hot gossip of the moment. As a manager, I knew the wounds would fester in other areas and with other people she would give her opinion of me to. I had to address it instead of waiting for it to die down as other managers might have done, which would have resulted in acrimonious meetings in the future. I was proactive in reaching out and making sure the meeting happened. I had a non-threatening meeting on her turf and initiated it by setting the goals for our time together.

Savvy leaders know how to call things out in a thoughtful way, as well as when not to address an issue. They see beyond the meeting and try not to take things personally. Their ultimate goal, dear reader, for every leader, regardless of the problem, should be to work towards building and nurturing strong relationships in the workplace.

BE ACCESSIBLY HUMAN

Remember to bring a human element to your role. You're not just a title, or "up and comer" or someone with a nice office wearing nice clothes. It's okay to be different than your peers in how you interact. I'm not suggesting you become the class clown, of course; but I am saying that just because Mr. Smith always eats alone with his door closed, shouldn't mean you need to follow that example. Get to the cafeteria and network! Take advantage of *Dress Down Friday* and don't wear a suit, wear what makes you comfortable – complete with sneakers.

If you spend one minute in my office you'll know that I love the Tampa Bay Lightning. If you get in my car and a playlist starts, you'll know I listen to heavy metal. I don't hide that. It has nothing to do with me performing my duties admirably. Outside of work I'm a human being...and I'm still me when I'm at work as well.

Savvy leadership is more attainable than you might believe. As with the other critical leadership skills I'm sharing in this book, this one requires intentional focus to be successful. You can make it happen!

CHAPTER 10
LIFE IS A TEAM SPORT

"HEY, COACH!"

Few titles, if any, have lost their luster more than *coach*. Forgive me if I sound like my grandfather for a moment; I have to – Back in my day (there it is!), a coach was primarily thought of as the top dog of a sports team. Coaches were respected by players at all levels, from kindergarten through the professional ranks. It was, and still is, a fantastic achievement to become a coach, to implement your system, your game plan, call the plays, and lead a team. The difference is, nowadays, we have coaches for everything.

We have sports coaches, relationship coaches, family coaches, physical (trainers) coaches, mental health coaches, spiritual coaches, business coaches, finance coaches, sales coaches, leadership coaches, performance coaches, and the list goes on and on.

I believe all of them are important. Being accountable to someone else can take you to the level you strive to achieve. Coaching is a billion-dollar industry, and it should be. Good coaches provide valuable information to their clients that can shorten the time frame it takes for them to reach their goals.

I myself have a variety of coaches including a personal trainer and nutrition coach—and they are an incredible asset to my health, which passes over to my mind and soul. However, there is a different set of coaches in my life that's also invaluable to me, but the major difference about these coaches is - they don't even know about it! I call them my Personal Board of Directors.

PERSONAL BOARD OF DIRECTORS

I firmly believe life is a team sport. That's not a glib statement; I genuinely believe it and say it constantly. We can be a much more effective community by working together than by boot-strapping everything as individuals. There is a stereotype that praises *self-made* men and women, and deservedly so. However, I would bet that there would be many more *made* individuals if they stopped trying to do everything themselves, especially when it's so easy to get help/advice/mentorship/coaching in this hyper-connected world.

As you have read by now, I am not risk adverse. I have made drastic career moves, including interviewing for and getting positions that I was not qualified for on paper. That being said, while it may look from the outside that I was operating as a Lone Ranger, I secretly had a group of people that were guiding me, pointing out blind spots, and forcing me to look within to see if where I wanted to go was consistent with who I was and, just as important, who I wanted to be.

Having a personal board of directors is not my original idea. I first heard it many years ago from my friend Charlie Judy. I immediately loved the concept; having a team of people to help me operate individually as if I were some non-profit or large corporation appealed to me on many levels. I have operational-ized it ever since.

Toward the end of each calendar year, I identify four or five people that can help me in the upcoming year. I don't just pick them willy-nilly; I don't put names in a hat and hope that the randomness of the universe comes through. And I certainly don't put names on a wall and throw darts to see which ones I hit. This is what I do...

I choose from folks I respect and that I'm already connected to. These people are not necessarily best friends, although, at times, some are very near and dear to me, and they also don't work in the same organization as I do. This is important because I don't want them to have a preconceived bias on a person, policy, business unit, or the organization's corporate culture. I don't want them to feel a burden of responsibility, so I don't have annual board retreats or once-a-month meetings as most boards do.

The most intriguing element of those I select for my Personal Board of Directors for the upcoming year is this: they have no idea they are on it!

Therein lies the power! When I've had to make major decisions, such as a job change or whether to implement an innovative style or system that could potentially disrupt the flow of business until it catches on, I've leaned into them and they have been an amazing sounding board. Because they have no idea they're on my board they unilaterally help me decipher if the move I'm considering makes sense without the pressure to 'sound good' in front of the others.

I'm smart enough to know that I don't know everything. I have, however, taken the time to do the introspective work to try to know myself better. That is not easy. One thing I've realized, and maybe you're a little like me, is that when I'm excited about something, it's easy to miss specific details or potential repercussions. I have been guilty of focusing my vision on the big thing and have missed obvious roadblocks. The complex work relationships or political issues in the "office" that can bias my decision-making doesn't impact my board of directors.

Their perspective, free from my biases, allows me to accept their suggestions, constructive criticism, and feedback with an open mind. Let's face it, you can get the best advice in the world, but if you aren't open to receiving it, it will be wasted wisdom. I have benefitted greatly from these trusted voices. I'm telling you, dear reader, this is priceless; where's your highlighter?

My best example, of many, is when I considered making a major career move away from a twenty-year career as an HR Executive at well-respected hospitals to leading the national health care practice for a human resources strategy and recruitment process outsourcing firm. It was a gargantuan decision and it felt... heavy. Although I was excited and intrigued with the prospect of moving into a consulting role, I was scared to death of leaving hospital-life where I was comfortable, confident, well supported, and respected. I was at the top of my game, and this move felt like starting over. That was scary!

Who did I turn to? My Board, of course. I described why I needed to leave my hospital executive life, and what this massive new responsibility could mean. I didn't want to sway their opinion either way. I asked them if they wouldn't mind helping me talk through it. The results were fantastic, honest conversations that provoked and challenged me. Ultimately, I decided to make that quantum leap in my career and accept the opportunity to move into the consulting world with much greater confidence than I would have had otherwise.

My Board has helped me personally and professionally over the years. They have changed the trajectory of my career for the better. I humbly submit to you, dear reader, to consider developing your own Board of Directors to help you navigate life's challenges and opportunities.

GET YOUR OWN BOARD!

You may be as intrigued about this concept as I was when I first heard of it. If so, you're probably thinking, *how can I find four or five people to be on MY personal board?* Everyone is different, so I will not put a once-size-fits-all recipe on whom to look for. I will, however, show you mine:

1. They can't work in the same organization you do.
2. They are familiar with your work and leadership style, so the feedback given won't be taken out of context and will feel natural to execute.
3. Since I'm an avid social media user, 75% of my personal board comes from relationships I cultivated on social media platforms. I have never met some in person! However, they know me through a different lens than most. Most likely, they know how strongly I feel about leadership because they know I have nearly 1,000 blog posts on the subject.

It's essential for me to find people in formal executive or other leadership roles. They know the nuances of how organizations operate without requiring explanation, thus granting them insight others may not possess.

I want to be clear; I'm not saying that if you want to be a Senior VP you should exclusively take a current Senior VP for coffee and pick their brain once a month for six months as your only strategy. That person is in effect serving as a sort of mentor. Additionally, an executive coach can be a powerful investment as you move throughout your career, one that I highly recommend and would be honored to serve as for you. A Personal Board, however, is a different, and contemporary supplemental approach.

What I'm saying is that God - the universe - a higher power, has placed people around you that have wisdom, insight, and experience who are willing to help talk you through difficult situations. They may not share your faith, they may not dress like you, and they may not even live in the same country – that doesn't matter. I may be the only one on my board who listens to heavy metal. What matters is if you can trust them to steer you clear from troubled waters and see a more clear vision of the path ahead you will benefit greatly.

If, like me, you can accept that you don't know everything, I suggest you recruit a Personal Board of Directors. Remember, life is a team sport, if you play it alone, you're at a severe disadvantage, but with the right team on your side, the sky is the limit.

CHAPTER 11
FEAR AND DECISION MAKING

DON'T FEAR, FEAR

I remember making a mistake in front of my team and instead of finding a way to look good or save face, I said, "Oh my goodness, I blew that one! Do I make that same mistake every Tuesday?" My team didn't put me down, laugh at me, or put me on a spit and cook me medium-well. On the contrary, the response was more like, "You're fine."

Too many wanna-be leaders are afraid of not being the most intelligent person in the room. They consciously or subconsciously hire people they feel won't become competition for their job. That is one of the deadly sins of leadership. If you were a racehorse, you should be put out to pasture. Or, at the very least, be taken out of the rat race and moved to the sidelines.

A high-energy leader serious about driving positive change must overcome the fear that someone on his or her team will look more competent. If you have a super high-achiever, highly influential, or knowledgeable person on your team, you need to understand it makes you look better. You're the one who hired and/or is developing that person! Immature leaders are threatened by smarter people. Please note, in this context, I don't use the word immature as having anything to do with a person's age; I'm referring to their mentality.

Fear and ego are a lethal combination, and leaders who suffer from both often make excuses as high potential members of their teams exit the organization. If you understood how much effort it takes to attract top-tier talent, you'd know how catastrophic these departures could be, primarily when those bright minds leave for a competitor.

Many micromanagers (regardless of their level in the organization) hire low(er) to ensure they are the smartest member of the team. That's ridiculous. Surround yourself with brilliant minds so that your team can do incredible work. Give them the freedom to ask questions and make suggestions and let them do what they do best. Being a micromanager, like being a helicopter parent, will never allow your team members to give you the best they can offer. Not everyone wants your job, but everyone wants to contribute, feel respected and grow.

I make sure to avoid taking credit for what a team member proposes. If I introduce a new concept that Laura, Mike, or Jane came up with, I'll say it in the meeting.

"Ok, so Jane came up with a great idea..."

I need to make sure Jane gets the credit she deserves. I need Jane to stay with my organization and, selfishly, with me. She makes the team better and, as a result, ultimately makes me look better. I can't stand when leaders take the credit they don't deserve. Smart, ambitious people leave organizations led by people like that. Every. Singe. Day.

DECISION MAKING

As I've shared throughout this book, I took risks and was promoted rapidly as a young professional. One day I was in an entry-level position, and then through a series of calculated risks, I managed employees. I was barely 30 years old, managing people the age of my parents. I was deathly afraid that I was over my head, but I didn't focus on the fear, I focused on the opportunity.

I smile when I think about how hard I suited up to go to work and the many poses I did in front of the mirror to find the ones that would make me look most managerial. People much older than me and with more hospital experience were now looking to me for answers. I had a choice to make – take it slow and learn the nooks and crannies of my surroundings or make decisions quickly and learn on the job. If you know me by now, you know I started making quick, impactful decisions.

One brief example: of the earliest decisions I made was simplifying the application process. In short, it was too long, and quite frankly, it sucked. I asked the woman who handled it to tell me about the process. I came to find out those applications were passed around in human resources nine times before they went to a hiring manager. I looked at the flow chart and drew a big "X" between steps 2 and 8, eliminating them.

"Are you going to just change that?" she asked.

"I believe we just did."

As you may well imagine, the people responsible for steps 2 through 8 did not like that they were cut out of the process. I was confronted and told I didn't know what I was doing. "I've been here for 30 years, and here you come, shaking everything up!"

Inside, I knew this was an early defining moment of my time as Vice President. However, on the outside, wearing my form-fitting suit and posturing up with one of my power poses, I knew I looked like I belonged, now, I had to act like it.

"That's because no one has had the courage to try new things. That's not how to become the number one hospital in the city, let alone the country. Let's make this happen together. I need you; we have work to do, and we all know this process no longer works."

If you fear making decisions, you don't belong in leadership. Honestly, what does "let me take a look at that?" mean? Stop circling back, tabling the discussion, and putting off vital decisions that need to be made. You get paid to make decisions! Stop being so safe and stop being so conservative. You have the potential to initiate change, create culture, and develop an identity for the employees. Stagnant organizations are those whose leaders put bumpers around their decisions, trying to mitigate a mistake they haven't made.

Analysis paralysis exists! The term is used too often, but for good reason; too many leaders are scared to offend anyone, so they would rather take in more information than decide on a course of action. Leaders across the globe who suffer from analysis paralysis choke the creativity, innovation and fun out of work and hold back the organization's growth. If you don't get comfortable making tough decisions, you will hit a career ceiling, regardless of the other great skills you may possess.

Executive level leaders are supposed to be decision makers, and rightfully so. They decide on the most critical business issues, such as the budget, potential expansion, reduction of force, mergers, and so on. Those roles are for people well-versed at decision making. Among their many other skill sets, they should be bold and be willing to make the right decision for the organization even if half of the workforce won't understand and get angry with them.

I know this is a "business leadership" book, but when it comes to decisions, allow me to go a bit deeper into your personal life. I want this book to speak to you. I dare say that there are unmade decisions you've been afraid to resolve, and it has held your joy of life back and compromised your quality of life. Yes, I said it.

Stop hitting the snooze button on the big decisions you have been afraid to make. You know what to do to build stronger relationships. You know what to do to be healthier. You know what to do to be happier. Make the decision and pull the trigger already. We only have one go-round at this beautiful thing called life.

Make the decisions you've been avoiding, personally and professionally, and let fear know you've won.

CHAPTER 12
IT'S YOUR MOVE

I want to congratulate you on getting this far into the book. I trust it has opened your eyes to new ways of thinking about your leadership style. However, and I say this with the utmost respect, dear reader – chances are, this is not the first book of this sort (leadership/self-development) you've read. Most people who read these books also attend conferences and lectures on leadership and personal growth. It could be true that you are reading this book because you never implemented great ideas and strategies you've learned from other books or people.

My question to you is this: what will you do with the knowledge you've learned from these pages?

If you know you're not going to try to leverage the power of energy, risk, and relationships – you may want to do someone a favor and gift this book to them so they can take action.

However, if you're ready to commit to becoming the leader you have always envisioned and are willing to adopt my three core elements of leadership, please read on.

I can't wait for you to turn the page and dive into the next chapter. Until now, I've been teaching and laying the foundation to put it all together - the very essence of this book.

Now let's finish strong!

CHAPTER 13
THE THREE MAJOR LEADERSHIP ELEMENTS – PLUS ONE!

THE BIG THREE

At the end of the day, you're not a leader if no one follows you. Combining my three major elements of leadership: Energy, Risk, and Relationships is how to achieve that goal. Let me put this all together for you as our time together draws to a close.

Energy is first, not that it's the most important, they are each essential. However, energy is first because, as we all know, high-energy people attract people. Great leaders know this and are adept at leveraging the power of attraction. Oftentimes it's hard to describe the infectiousness of people that ooze good energy. Charismatic leaders have an abundance of people that want to be on their team. I'm not talking about over-the-top, cheesy, obnoxious salesmanship charisma – I'm referring to a genuine, great smile, great eye contact, pep-in-your-step, confident, caring, and empathetic charisma.

Think of a leader with the opposite traits, low energy and talks like they are always tired, as they often slump their shoulders in a sign of resignation to the world's pressure. People will listen if they are under that type of leadership because they have to, but they're certainly not inspired, they don't love coming to work, they don't go the extra mile, in fact, it's hard enough for them to stay awake during meetings. I can't stress this enough, some extraordinary leaders are introverts. The energy I teach has nothing to do with if you're an intro or extravert – it's about being passionately present.

Next is Risk. Find the courage to take risks. I'm not saying to make irresponsible decisions because you have not done your due diligence. What I am saying, however, is that once you've received the available data, make a decision! We don't have crystal balls to show us what decisions to make, but you do have to make them. It could be trying something that's never been done, having a temporary partnership with a competitor, or championing a technology or ideology as an early adopter.

Then there are Relationships. Cultivating great relationships requires both energy and risk. Relationships can't grow if you don't invest energy on them. Often, there's a level of risk involved in solidifying a relationship because you may have to show your vulnerable side. Regardless of where people are on the corporate ladder, showing them that they matter is so important. Job titles and pay grades be damned. Each person is valuable. Make sure they know that you know.

Much like people follow and feel connected to celebrities on social media, thinking they know their values, philosophies, and who they are as a person; the same experience happens for leaders at all levels. It's okay. Learn to be comfortable in the leadership limelight. Having hundreds or thousands of people in an organization think they know your personal life is always risky, but it can be a powerful lynchpin for having strong, healthy working relationships.

If you integrate my three elements of leadership into your style, you'll put yourself in the best position to reach your leadership goals.

If your sole focus is on energy, people will see significant gaps in your leadership skills. If you're somewhat risk-averse (afraid of making tough decisions) and don't put the energy into having people share your vision, you will never make the impact you desire.

If you focus exclusively on high energy but actually only care about the company's financial goals and don't invest in relationships, you'll not have the support you need to push your ideas through. Independent of each other, you'll hit the ceiling of your career and soon start to slide down the corporate ladder.

However, when the three are intertwined, the sky's the limit – especially if you combine it with a fourth element. That's right. There's a bonus element!

THE FOUNDATION OF A STRONG MORAL COMPASS.

I've had a visual concept of a "values filter" for years. When I make major and some not-so-major decisions, I filter them through my personal values, which act as my moral compass. If it can pass through that filter, which is anchored on my faith, I feel great about it. At the end of the day, leaders make many decisions; for me, having a clear conscience about the tough decisions I have to make allows me to sleep well at night.

That doesn't mean my decisions will be popular or readily accepted, but I'll know in my heart it's the best decision based on the data available, as well as it's what my heart tells me should be done. The truth is this, when I have to make decisions and I step back and take into account the three major leadership elements, and it passes my moral compass test, it will have a much greater chance to be effective, even if the implementation might be challenging.

Let me take a moment and expand on the impact of applying a moral compass in the workplace. Employees and leaders of all levels have reached out to me and shared their most confidential/personal issues, such as their fragile employment status, sexual harassment, impending divorces, low personal funds, and affairs – you name it. I don't tell them about my moral compass but they have sensed it. They knew they could trust me and ask for my guidance because they'd witnessed first-hand how I conducted myself. It has been incredibly humbling to be thought of in that way. They knew that I valued and respected them as equal members of the organization.

Conversely, the opposite is true. People who are shown to be unethical, manipulative, and have abused their authority, whether great or small, ran from me. They didn't want to interact with me. They knew that if they appeared on my radar, I would not stay silent. They knew I would hold them accountable. I have felt just as pleased when unethical folks are nervous around me as when others have approached me for support or counsel.

My question to you, dear reader, is this: what drives your moral compass? What set of values have you set as non-negotiable? Is it faith? A personal standard? Have you never considered one? If so, I urge you to consider it now. What are the non-negotiables for you? How will you protect the innocent in the workplace from others with more authority? Find your moral compass and let it guide you. Trust me, it will be evident to others, even if they don't know it.

One day, while staying at the office late, a worker from our environmental services team came to clean and vacuum my office. I stopped what I was doing and chatted with him for a few minutes, as I often did. When he left, he said, "I really appreciate the type of person you are. I can tell you're a man of God."

My jaw just about hit the floor! I had never shared my faith perspective with him. I didn't have scripture posted in my office. Still, somehow, he was able to discern, through my behavior, the core of what guides me. He detected that I valued relationships and that I treat everyone equally. In short, he noticed that the moral compass inside of me was alive and well.

I didn't share that story to brag in any way. It's a deeply personal one I questioned leaving in this book. I decided to keep it here because I try to practice what I preach about relationships and humanizing myself as a leader. It's important for you to do that as well.

12 MONTHS FROM NOW

I have a challenge for you. Now that we're at the end of our time together, I'd like you to close your eyes for a moment and envision yourself twelve months from now after having intentionally applied the three major leadership elements of energy, risk, and relationships, and had your decisions filtered through your moral compass. How does your leadership career look? Did you move ahead? Did you move to another organization in an expanded role?

As you envision your best self a year from now after applying what I taught here, ask yourself, what do your employees say about you? What changed? Did you make a risky move that panned out for the organization? How did they thank you? Do people walk up to you in the hallway to say hi and shake your hand as they walk by, or do they still look down and walk past you without even a nod?

Whether you think incorporating the three major leadership elements plus the bonus one is easy or not, I want you to know that it's definitely doable and worthy of your efforts. Your best life is tied to your professional life; you can't have one without the other. Life is better when you stack wins. If you can stack wins in your leadership style; success, abundance, and confidence will permeate to other areas of your life.

Even though we're at the end of our time together, I have good news. Closing this book does not have to mean we can't be connected. I'm passionate about helping leaders grow and evolve, and I'd love to continue the dialogue with you going forward. Please use me as a resource. The world is complicated enough, and leading the world of work is a tremendous burden. However, I'm willing to support you and remind you that leading others is also a privilege.

Let's follow each other on social channels.

Allow me the opportunity to speak at your event.

Reach out for coaching support.

Let's connect at http://www.jaykuhns.com.

Join my community and let's be the leaders our colleagues and organizations need. You deserve it and they deserve the best you.

You can make it happen!

ABOUT THE AUTHOR

Jay Kuhns is a human resources executive, leadership coach, speaker, consultant and is the author of Unstoppable Power, Leverage Energy, Risk and Relationships and Advance Your Leadership Career.

For more than twenty-five years Jay's progressive leadership approach has propelled him to executive positions with the Johns Hopkins Health System, HCA, and several consulting firms. His leadership blog NoExcusesHR, which he has written for more than a decade, has consistently been recognized for its high accountability focus on leadership.

Jay lives in Tampa, Florida where he volunteers on the Board of the Children's Cancer Center and in various leadership positions at Hyde Park United Methodist Church. In his free time, he enjoys every minute with his family, friends and cheering on the Tampa Bay Lightning.

ACKNOWLEDGMENTS

Writing a book is a significant personal accomplishment; yet it requires an army of support...at least it did for me. Please allow me to thank some of those who helped make *Unstoppable Power* come to life.

First and foremost, you would not be reading this if it wasn't for the amazing team at The Ghost Publishing: Eli Gonzalez, Michelle Schacht, and Blair Towney. Eli, you, and your team have been incredible. Thank you, my friend!

My parents Gary and Janet Kuhns. Your love and support throughout this process (and from above Dad) has been amazing. There isn't a more fortunate son than me.

My kids, Audrey and Mitch Conyers, Jeff Kuhns and Gary Kuhns for not only being excited for me to take on this project, but to show so much love and genuine interest in what their dad was up to.

My sister Julie Kuhns and her husband David Moulton. You never wavered in your support and enthusiasm.

My friend Patrick Moraites who brought a level of inspiration and encouragement that only a best friend could do. Thank you, brother.

My friend Jeff Gigante for encouraging me to go for it, and for introducing me to the best writing team in the business.

My friend and colleague Gordon Tredgold. Our connection was immediate, and I cannot thank you enough for your time, insight, and humbling foreword to *Unstoppable Power*.

My dear friends and colleagues David Cook, Steve Browne, Tina Suojanen, Mike Wukitsch, Lotus Buckner, Mamoon Syed, Kim Pope, Charlie Judy, and Ron Thomas for your contribution to this project and the incredible words of support.

My pal who is the man behind my look and the camera too, Rey Jijon.

My longtime friend and the brainpower behind jaykuhns.com Darrell Lee.

My colleagues who continue to be nothing but positive as I launch this project. Your support means more than you know.

To my good friend Magrey deVega and my bible study brothers for your thoughtful words of encouragement.

And Erin Jones. You have walked this journey with me every step of the way and have been nothing short of incredible. We have so much more ahead. Thank you from the bottom of my heart.

www.ingramcontent.com/pod-product-compliance
Lightning Source LLC
Chambersburg PA
CBHW060337130626

46553CB00003B/1036